Instant Pot Cookbook.

Top 50+ Quick Easy and Healthy Recipes for Your
Electric Pressure Cooker.

Your Free Gift

I wanted to show my appreciation that you support my work so I've put together a free gift for you.

https://april4tale.wixsite.com/julianelsonsalads

Just visit the link above to download it now.

I know you will love this gift.

Thanks!

Julia Nelson

Table of Contents:

Introduction

In this day and age it's easier to grab ready-made food than cooking from scratch. A busy life schedule has badly impacted everyone's health. This is why people nowadays are trying to find the easier ways to eat healthy and stay healthy. An instant pot is the solution to all these problems.

Instant pot is the latest addition to your kitchen mates designed by Canadians. It's a programmable pressure cooker that's safe, dependable and quite convenient to use. It uses 70% less energy and speeds up the cooking by no less than 2 to 6 times, so you don't need to spend ages in the kitchen to cook healthy food.

This is the ideal kitchen mate for a fast-paced and health-oriented lifestyle. Instant pot is a one pot multi-cooker capable of cooking multiple healthy foods for health conscious folks.

Instant pot is a smart and intelligent replacement of a rice cooker, pressure cooker and slow cooker. It preserves more nutrients as it takes less time cooking healthy foods than a slow cooker.

Benefits of Instant Pot

- *Absolutely dependable and safe to use*: with instant pot certified safety protection, it's safe to use even by the novice cooks.

- *Easy to clean*: it's quite easy to clean and pleasant to use. Absolutely quiet with no spills, no smell and no steam.

- *Energy saver*: it smartly saves energy up to 70%.

- *Convenient*: there are one-touch keys for most of the cooking tasks, and you can adjust cooking time according to your requirement. Slow cooking or quick meals, everything is possible with this miraculous kitchen gadget.

- *Health and nutrition*: it prepares healthy and nutritious foods consistently every time you use it.

51 Healthy Instant Pot Recipes

This book is finely illustrated with 51 healthy instant pot recipes that are low sodium with easy-to-buy fresh ingredients. You will find here healthy and scrumptious instant pot recipes for soups, stews, seafood, vegetables, grains, beans and desserts. **Enjoy!**

Soup, Stews & Chili Recipes

Soups and stews are hearty meals everyone craves during the fall and winter seasons. These are quite filling and healthy, too. Soups are considered great for weight loss and detoxing. They are indeed awesome to serve lean proteins and building muscles. Most of the soups and stews are dump meals as you dump everything in a stew pot, let it cook and you're done.

Tomato Soup

An easy way to prepare a wonderfully delicious tomato soup at home, tomatoes are an excellent source of healthy nutrients like vitamin C, vitamin K, copper, potassium, manganese and dietary fiber, etc. Garnishing with fresh basil also gives a refreshing touch to soup.

Yield: Makes 8 bowls
Cooking Time: 13 minutes

Ingredients:

- 1 tablespoon olive oil
- 1 medium onion, chopped
- 1 garlic clove, minced
- 3 pound fresh tomatoes, chopped
- 2 tablespoons homemade tomato sauce
- 2 teaspoons dried parsley, crushed
- 2 teaspoons dried basil, crushed
- Freshly ground black pepper, to taste
- 3½ cups low-sodium vegetable broth
- 2 tablespoons sugar
- 1 tablespoon balsamic vinegar
- ¼ cup fresh basil, chopped

Directions

1. Pour the oil in the Instant Pot and select "Sauté." Add the onion and garlic and cook for about 3 minutes.

2. Select the "Cancel" button and stir in the tomatoes, homemade tomato sauce, herbs, black pepper and broth. Next, secure the lid and select "Soup" and just use the default time of 10 minutes. Select the "Cancel" and carefully do a quick release.

3. Remove the lid and stir in the sugar and vinegar. With an immerse blender, puree the soup.

4. Serve immediately with the garnishing of basil.

Potato & Corn Soup

Yield: Makes 8 bowls
Cooking Time: 12 minutes

Ingredients

- 2 tablespoons unsalted butter
- 3 carrots, peeled and chopped
- 2 celery stalks, chopped
- 1 medium onion, chopped
- 2 garlic cloves, chopped finely
- 2 large russet potatoes, peeled and chopped
- 2 cups fresh corn kernels
- 2 tablespoons dried parsley, crushed
- Freshly ground black pepper, to taste
- 6 cups low-sodium vegetable broth
- 3 tablespoons cornstarch
- ¼ cup half-and-half

Directions

1. Place the butter in the Instant Pot and select "Sauté." Add the carrot, celery, onion and garlic and cook for about 3-4 minutes.

2. Select the "Cancel" button and stir in the potatoes, corn kernels, parsley, black pepper and broth. Next, secure the lid and cook under "Manual" and "High Pressure" for about 5 minutes. Select the "Cancel" button and carefully do a natural release for about 10 minutes and then do a quick release.

3. Meanwhile, in a bowl, dissolve the cornstarch in half-and-half.

4. Remove the lid from the Instant Pot and add the cornstarch mixture into the soup, stirring continuously. Select "Sauté" and cook for about 3 minutes more.

5. Serve immediately.

Chicken & Kale Soup

A hearty soup packed with super nutritious ingredients like chicken, kale, carrots, etc. Kale is considered one of the healthiest foods, as it's loaded with all sorts of vital nutrients. You can prepare this hearty soup in an Instant Pot in less than 15 minutes.

Yield: Makes 4 bowls
Cooking Time: 12 minutes

Ingredients

- 2 tablespoons olive oil
- 4 celery stalks, chopped
- 3 carrots, peeled and chopped
- 1 medium onion, chopped
- 2 bay leaves
- ¼ teaspoon dried oregano, crushed
- ¼ teaspoon dried thyme, crushed
- Freshly ground black pepper, to taste
- 4 cups low-sodium chicken broth
- 1 cup water
- 1 pound cooked chicken, shredded
- 2 cups fresh kale, trimmed and chopped
- ½ teaspoon Worcestershire sauce

Directions

1. Pour the oil in the Instant Pot and select "Sauté." Add the celery, carrot and onion, and cook for about 5 minutes. Add bay leaves, herbs and black pepper, and cook for about 1 minute.

2. Select the "Cancel" button and stir in the broth and water. Next, secure the lid and select "Soup," and just use the default time of 4 minutes. Select the "Cancel" button and carefully do a quick release.

3. Remove the lid and stir in the chicken and kale. Select "Sauté" and cook for about 1-2 minutes more.

4. Stir in Worcestershire sauce and serve immediately.

Beef & Green Bean Soup

Yield: Makes 6 bowls
Cooking Time: 38 minutes

Ingredients

- 1 tablespoon olive oil
- 1 pound lean ground beef
- 1 medium onion, chopped
- 1 tablespoon garlic, minced
- 2 teaspoons dried thyme, crushed
- 1 teaspoon ground cumin
- 3 cups fresh tomatoes, chopped finely
- ½ pound fresh green beans, trimmed and cut into 1-inch pieces
- 4¼ cups low-sodium beef broth
- Freshly ground black pepper, to taste
- ¼ cup Parmesan cheese, grated freshly

Directions

1. Pour the oil in the Instant Pot and select "Sauté." Add the beef and cook for about 5 minutes or until browned completely. Add onion, garlic, thyme, and cumin, and cook for about 3 minutes.

2. Select the "Cancel" button and stir in the tomatoes, beans and broth. Next, secure the lid and cook under "Manual" and "Low Pressure" for about 30 minutes. Select the "Cancel" button and carefully do a quick release.

3. Remove the lid and stir in the black pepper.

4. Serve immediately with the garnishing of the Parmesan cheese.

Pork & Cabbage Soup

Yield: Makes 6 bowls
Cooking Time: 30 minutes

Ingredients

- 1 tablespoon olive oil
- 1 pound ground pork
- 1 large onion, chopped
- 2 cups carrots, peeled and shredded
- ½ head cabbage, chopped
- 4 cups low-sodium chicken broth
- 2/3 cup coconut aminos
- 1 teaspoon ground ginger
- Freshly ground black pepper, to taste

Directions

1. Pour the oil in the Instant Pot and select "Sauté." Then add the pork and cook for about 5 minutes or until browned completely.

2. Select "Cancel" and stir in the remaining ingredients. Next, secure the lid and cook under "Manual" and "High Pressure" for about 25 minutes. Select the "Cancel" button and carefully do a quick release.

3. Remove the lid and serve hot.

Chicken & Mushroom Stew

Yield: Makes 6 bowls
Cooking Time: 15 minutes

Ingredients

- 1 tablespoon olive oil
- 1 pound fresh cremini mushrooms, stemmed and quartered
- 1 small onion, chopped
- 1 tablespoon tomato paste
- 3 garlic cloves, minced
- 8 (5-ounce) skinless chicken thighs
- 1 cup green olives, pitted and halved
- 2 cups fresh cherry tomatoes
- ½ cup low-sodium chicken broth
- Freshly ground black pepper, to taste
- ½ cup fresh parsley, chopped

Directions

1. Pour the oil in the Instant Pot and select "Sauté." Add the mushrooms and onion, and cook for about 4-5 minutes. Add tomato paste and garlic, and cook for about 1 minute.

2. Select "Cancel" and stir in the chicken, olives, tomatoes and broth. Next, secure the lid and cook under "Manual" and "High Pressure" for about 9-10 minutes. Select the "Cancel" button and carefully do a quick release.

3. Remove the lid and stir in black pepper and parsley. Serve hot.

Beef & Veggie Stew

An ideal stew recipe for Instant Pot cooking, beef and veggies are braised in tomato sauce and broth in a delicious way. This filling stew is a great choice for chilly winter night dinners. Surely this stew will satisfy your tummy nicely.

Yield: Makes 8 bowls
Cooking Time: 50 minutes

Ingredients

- 3 tablespoons olive oil
- 2½ pound chuck roast, trimmed and cubed
- 2 cups homemade tomato sauce
- 1 teaspoon smoked paprika
- 2 cups low-sodium chicken broth
- 2 large onions, cut into bite sized pieces
- 1 pound carrots, peeled and cut into bite sized pieces
- 1 pound potatoes, peeled and cut into bite sized pieces
- 1 garlic clove, minced
- ½ cup fresh cilantro, chopped

Directions

1. Pour the oil in the Instant Pot and select "Sauté." Add the beef and cook for about 5 minutes.

2. Select "Cancel" and stir in the tomato paste, paprika and broth. Next, secure the lid and cook under "Manual" and "High Pressure" for about 15 minutes. Once finished, carefully do a quick release.

3. Select the "Cancel" button and stir in the vegetables. Secure the lid and cook under "Manual" and "High Pressure" for about 30 minutes. Select the "Cancel" button and carefully do a quick release.

4. Remove the lid and stir in the cilantro. Serve hot.

Mixed Veggie Stew

Yield: Makes 10 bowls
Cooking Time: 26 minutes

Ingredients

- 2 tablespoons olive oil
- 1 carrot, peeled and minced
- 1 celery stalk, minced
- 1 small onion, minced
- 2 garlic cloves, minced
- 1 teaspoon dried sage, crushed
- 1 teaspoon dried rosemary, crushed
- 8-ounce fresh Portabella mushrooms, sliced
- 8-ounce fresh white mushrooms, sliced
- ½ cup red wine
- 2 carrots, peeled and chopped
- 2 Yukon Gold potatoes, peeled and chopped
- 1½ cups fresh green beans, trimmed and chopped
- 2 cups tomatoes, chopped
- 1 cup homemade tomato paste
- 1 tablespoon balsamic vinegar
- 3 cups water
- 2 tablespoons cornstarch
- ¼ cup water
- Salt and freshly ground black pepper, to taste
- 4-ounce frozen peas
- ¾ cup pearl onion

Directions

1. Pour the oil in the Instant Pot and select "Sauté." Add the carrot, celery and onion, and cook for about 2-3 minutes. Add garlic and herbs and cook for about 1 minute. Add mushrooms and cook for about 4-5 minutes. Add the wine and cook for about 2 minutes, scraping the brown bits from the bottom.

2. Select "Cancel" and stir in the carrots, potatoes, green beans, tomatoes, tomato paste, vinegar and water. Next, secure the lid and cook under "Manual" and "High Pressure" for about 15 minutes. Select the "Cancel" button and carefully do a quick release.

3. Meanwhile, in a bowl, dissolve the cornstarch into water.

4. Remove the lid of the Instant Pot and immediately stir in the cornstarch mixture, salt, black pepper, peas and pearl onions. Select "Sauté" and cook for about 1 minute.

5. Serve hot.

Chicken & Corn Chili

Yield: Makes 4 bowls
Cooking Time: 18 minutes

Ingredients

- 2 tablespoons olive oil
- 1¼ cups onion, hopped
- 2 teaspoons garlic, minced
- 3½ cups cooked chicken, chopped
- 2 cups tomatoes, chopped finely
- 2/3 cup jalapeño peppers, seeded and chopped
- 1 teaspoon dried oregano, crushed
- 2 teaspoons red chili powder
- 1 teaspoon ground cumin
- 2½ cups low-sodium chicken broth
- 14-ounce fresh corn kernel
- 8-ounce cream cheese, softened
- 1 cup cooked bacon, chopped, divided
- ½ cup Pepper Jack cheese, shredded

Directions

1. Pour the oil in the Instant Pot and select "Sauté." Then add the onion and cook for about 5 minutes.

2. Select "Cancel" and stir in the remaining ingredients except cream cheese, bacon and Pepper Jack cheese. Next, secure the lid and select "Soup" and just use the

default time of 10 minutes. Select the "Cancel" button and carefully do a quick release.

3. Remove the lid and stir in the cream cheese and a ½ cup of the bacon. Select "Sauté" and cook for about 3 minutes.Top with the remaining bacon and Pepper Jack cheese and serve hot.

Beef & Beans Chili

Yield: Makes 8 bowls
Cooking Time: 23 minutes

Ingredients

- 1 tablespoon olive oil
- 2 pound ground beef
- 1 onion, chopped
- 1 green bell pepper, seeded and chopped
- 2 garlic cloves, minced
- 1 teaspoon dried oregano, crushed
- 3 tablespoons red chili powder
- 1 tablespoon ground cumin
- 3½ cups tomatoes, chopped finely
- 1½ cups cooked red kidney beans
- 1½ cups water
- ½ cup sour cream

Directions

1. Pour the oil in the Instant Pot and select "Sauté."

2. Add the beef and cook for about 5 minutes or until browned completely. With a slotted spoon, transfer the beef into a bowl. Drain the excess grease from the pot, leaving about 1 tablespoon. Now, add the onion and bell pepper and cook for about 4 minutes. Add the garlic, oregano and spices, and cook for about 1 minute. Add tomatoes and cook for about 2 minutes, crushing with the back of a spoon.

3. Select "Cancel" and stir in the remaining ingredients except sour cream. Next, secure the lid and cook under "Manual" and "High Pressure" for about 10 minutes. Select the "Cancel" button and carefully do a quick release.

4. Remove the lid.Top with sour cream and serve hot.

Three Beans Chili

One of the best and most delicious vegetarian chilis, this dish will be a great meal for vegetarians and meat lovers alike. A balanced combo of spices is the main key to the delicious flavors of this chili. Instant Pot prepares this delicious chili for your dinner in just under 20 minutes.

Yield: Makes 8 bowls
Cooking Time: 17 minutes

Ingredients

For Chili

- 2 tablespoons olive oil
- 2 cups onion, chopped
- 1 green bell pepper, seeded and chopped
- ¾ cup carrot, peeled and chopped
- ¼ cup celery stalk, chopped
- 1 tablespoon garlic, minced
- 2/3 cup dried kidney beans, rinsed, soaked for 8 hours and drained
- 2/3 cup dried pinto beans, rinsed, soaked for 8 hours and drained
- 2/3 cup dried black beans, rinsed, soaked for 8 hours and drained
- 2 cups fresh tomatoes, chopped
- 2 cups homemade tomato paste
- 2 teaspoons dried oregano, crushed
- 2 tablespoons mild chili powder
- 1 teaspoon smoked paprika

- ¼ teaspoon cayenne pepper
- 1½ teaspoons ground cumin
- ½ teaspoon ground coriander
- 3½ cups low-sodium vegetable broth

For Topping

- ½ cup scallion, chopped
- ½ cup black olives, pitted and sliced

Directions

1. For chili, pour the oil in the Instant Pot and select "Sauté." Then add the onion, bell pepper, carrot, celery and garlic, and cook for about 4-5 minutes.

2. Select "Cancel" and stir in the remaining ingredients. Next, secure the lid and cook under "Manual" and "High Pressure" for about 12-15 minutes. Select the "Cancel" button and carefully do a natural release.

3. Remove the lid.Top with scallions and olives, and then serve hot.

Meat & Poultry Recipes

Meats only taste great if nicely cooked to your desired doneness. And that tenderness and juiciness is successfully achieved using the Instant Pot. These Instant Pot recipes will give you ultimate satisfaction combined with great taste and health.

Beef with Mushroom Gravy

Yield: Makes 6 plates
Cooking Time: 1 hour 7 minutes

Ingredients

For Beef

- 3½ pound beef chuck roast, trimmed and cubed into 2-inch size
- 3 garlic cloves, minced
- 1 tablespoon mixed dried herbs, crushed (of your choice)
- Freshly ground white pepper, to taste
- 2 tablespoons unsalted butter
- 1 onion, chopped
- 2 cups low-sodium beef broth
- ¼ cup red wine
- 4 large carrots, peeled and cut into 1-inch pieces

For Gravy

- 4 tablespoons unsalted butter
- 4-ounce cremini mushrooms, sliced
- ½ teaspoon dried thyme, crushed
- ¼ cup red wine
- ½ cup sour cream

Directions

1. Add beef, garlic, mixed herbs and white pepper to a bowl and toss to coat well.

2. Place the butter in the Instant Pot and select "Sauté." Add the onion and cook for about 4-5 minutes. Add the wine and cook for about 1-2 minutes, scraping the brown bits from the bottom.

3. Select the "Cancel" button and place the beef over the onion. Pour broth on top. Next, secure the lid and cook under "Manual" and "High Pressure" for about 40 minutes. Select the "Cancel" button and carefully do a quick release.

4. Remove the lid and stir in the carrot. Select "Sauté" and cook for about 10 minutes. Transfer the beef mixture into a large bowl and cover with a piece of foil to keep warm.

5. For gravy, place the butter in the Instant Pot and select "Sauté." Then add the mushrooms, thyme and wine and cook for about 10 minutes.

6. Select the "Cancel" button and stir in the sour cream.

7. Immediately, pour mushroom gravy over beef mixture and serve.

Beef Pot Roast

A classic recipe of beef for special family dinners, this succulent beef is prepared with garlic, apple, orange juice, broth and soy sauce. You can enjoy this shredded beef with pan sauce as a meal or it can be used in sandwiches, burgers and subs as well.

Yield: Makes 6 plates
Cooking Time: 50 minutes

Ingredients

- 2 tablespoons olive oil
- 4 pound beef bottom roast, cubed
- 1 cup low-sodium beef broth
- ½ cup low-sodium soy sauce
- 1 tablespoon fresh ginger, grated finely
- 5 garlic cloves, mince
- 1 Granny Smith apple, peeled, cored and chopped
- Freshly ground black pepper, to taste
- ¼ cup fresh orange juice

Directions

1. Pour the oil in the Instant Pot and select "Sauté." Add the beef cubes in batches and cook each batch for about 4-5 minutes.

2. Select "Cancel" and stir in the remaining ingredients. Next, secure the lid and cook under "Manual" and "Normal Pressure" for about 45 minutes.

3. Select the "Cancel" button and carefully do a quick release.

4. Remove the lid, and with 2 forks, shred the beef.

5. Serve hot with pan sauce.

Mongolian Beef

Yield: Makes 6 plates
Cooking Time: 18 minutes

Ingredients

- 1 tablespoon olive oil
- 2 pound flank steak, cut into ¼-inch strips
- 4 garlic cloves, minced
- ½ teaspoon fresh ginger, minced
- 2/3 cup dark brown sugar
- ½ cup water
- ½ cup low-sodium soy sauce
- 2 tablespoons cornstarch
- 3 tablespoons water
- 3 scallions, chopped

Directions

1. Pour the oil in the Instant Pot and select "Sauté." Add the beef strips in batches and cook each batch for about 5 minutes. Transfer the beef into a bowl. Add the garlic and ginger and cook for about 1 minute.

2. Select "Cancel" and stir in the remaining ingredients, except the scallions. Next, secure the lid and cook under "Manual" and "High Pressure" for about 12 minutes. Select the "Cancel" button and carefully do a quick release.

3. Remove the lid and stir in scallions.

4. Serve hot.

Spicy Pork Ribs

Yield: Makes 6 plates
Cooking Time: 40 minutes

Ingredients

- 2 garlic cloves, minced
- 1 teaspoon dried thyme, crushed
- 1 teaspoon smoked paprika
- ½ teaspoon ground cumin
- 12 teaspoon ground coriander
- ¼ teaspoon ground allspice
- Freshly ground black pepper, to taste
- 2½ pound boneless pork ribs
- 1 cup low-sodium chicken broth
- 1 cup homemade tomato sauce
- 2 tablespoons balsamic vinegar
- 2 teaspoons mustard powder
- 2 tablespoons olive oil
- 1 large onion, sliced

Directions

1. In a large bowl, mix together the garlic, thyme and spices. Add the pork ribs and coat with spice mixture generously. In another small bowl, mix together broth, tomato sauce, vinegar and mustard.
2. Pour the oil in the Instant Pot and select "Sauté." Add the onion and cook for about 4-5 minutes.
3. Select "Cancel" and place the pork over the ribs. Pour broth mixture over the ribs. Next, secure the lid and

38

select "Meat" and just use the default time of 35 minutes. Select the "Cancel" button and carefully do a natural release.

4. Remove the lid and serve immediately.

Fruity Pork Loin

One of the easiest ways to prepare a delicious meal in an Instant Pot, you can say that this meal is fuss-free cooking. Just dump all ingredients in your Instant Pot and select the "Meat" setting for a particular time. Open your pot and enjoy a hearty meal at the dinner table.

Yield: Makes 4 plates
Cooking Time: 40 minutes

Ingredients

- 1 1/3 pound boneless pork tenderloin
- 2 cups apples, cored and chopped
- 2/3 cup fresh cherries, pitted
- 1/3 cup celery stalk, chopped
- 1/3 cup onion, chopped
- ½ cup fresh apple juice
- Pinch of salt
- Freshly ground black pepper, to taste

Directions

1. Place all the ingredients in the Instant Pot and secure the lid. Select "Meat" and just use the default time of 40 minutes. Select the "Cancel" button and carefully do a quick release.
2. Remove the lid and serve immediately.

Lamb & Veggie Curry

Yield: Makes 6 bowls

Cooking Time: 39 minutes

Ingredients

- 2 tablespoons coconut oil
- 1 onion, chopped
- 1 teaspoon fresh ginger, minced
- 3 garlic cloves, minced
- 1 Serrano pepper, seeded and chopped
- 1 teaspoon ground coriander
- 1 teaspoon ground cumin
- 1 teaspoon red chili powder
- ¼ teaspoon ground turmeric
- 4 fresh tomatoes, chopped finely
- 1 pound ground lamb
- 3 carrots, peeled and chopped
- 2 potatoes, peeled and chopped
- 1 cup fresh peas, shelled
- 1½ cups homemade tomato sauce
- ½ cup unsweetened coconut milk
- ¼ cup fresh cilantro, chopped

Directions

1. Place the coconut oil in the Instant Pot and select "Sauté." Add the onion and garlic and cook for about 3 minutes. Add ginger, garlic, Serrano pepper and spices

and cook for about 1 minute. Add lamb and cook for about 5 minutes.

2. Select "Cancel" and stir in the remaining ingredients, except the cilantro. Next, secure the lid and select "Chili," using the default time of 30 minutes. Select the "Cancel" button and carefully do a natural release.

3. Remove the lid and stir in cilantro.

4. Serve hot.

Chicken Curry

Yield: Makes 8 bowls
Cooking Time: 23 minutes

Ingredients

For Spice Paste

- 6 shallots, chopped roughly
- 4 small dried red chilies
- ¾ cup unsweetened coconut, grated
- 1 teaspoon fennel seeds
- 1 teaspoon coriander seeds
- 1 teaspoon cumin seeds
- 1 teaspoon black pepper corns
- 1 teaspoon ground cinnamon
- 1 teaspoon ground turmeric
- ¼ cup water

For Chicken

- 1 tablespoon coconut oil
- 2 large onions, chopped
- 1 teaspoon fresh ginger, minced
- 2 garlic cloves, minced
- 2 large tomatoes, chopped
- 3 pound skinless, boneless chicken thighs, cubed
- 1 tablespoon fresh lemon juice
- Pinch of salt

- ½ cup fresh parsley, chopped

Directions

1. For the spice paste, add the shallots and dried chilies to the Instant Pot. Select "Sauté" and cook for about 2 minutes. Transfer the shallot mixture into a food processor. Add coconut and spices, and cook for about 1 minute. Select "Cancel" and transfer the spice mixture into the food processor with the shallot mixture. Add ¼ cup of water and pulse until a smooth paste forms.

2. Pour the oil in the Instant Pot and select "Sauté." Add the onion and cook for about 4-5 minutes. Add the ginger, garlic and spice paste and cook for about 2 minutes. Add tomatoes and cook for about 2-3 minutes.

4. Select "Cancel" and stir in the remaining ingredients, except the parsley. Next, secure the lid and cook under "Manual" and "High Pressure" for about 10 minutes. Select the "Cancel" button and carefully do a natural release.

3. Remove the lid and stir in parsley.

4. Serve hot.

Chicken with Pineapple

An easy and yummy way to have healthy protein with sweet pineapple, this Hawaiian style entrée meal will be a hit for the whole family. Chicken and pineapple pair nicely with sweet, sour and spicy coconut sauces.

Yield: Makes 4 plates
Cooking Time: 10 minutes

Ingredients

For Sauce

- ½ cup unsweetened coconut milk
- ½ cup homemade tomato sauce
- 2 tablespoons apple cider vinegar
- 2 tablespoons water
- 2 tablespoons brown sugar
- ½ teaspoon ground mustard
- 1 teaspoon red pepper flakes, crushed
- Pinch of salt
- Freshly ground black pepper, to taste

For Chicken

- 4 (6-ounce) chicken drumsticks, trimmed
- 1 cup fresh pineapple, chopped
- 1 tablespoon fresh lime juice

Directions

1. For sauce in a large bowl, mix together all ingredients. Add chicken drumsticks and coat with sauce generously.

2. In the bottom of the Instant Pot, place the chopped pineapple evenly. Arrange the drumsticks over the pineapple pieces in a single layer. Pour sauce over drumsticks evenly.

3. Next, secure the lid and cook under "Manual" and "High Pressure" for about 10 minutes. Select the "Cancel" button and carefully do a quick release.

4. Remove the lid and serve these drumsticks with the drizzling of lime juice.

Spicy Roasted Chicken

A surprisingly easy recipe of delicious roasted chicken, the fresh rosemary with spices adds a flavorsome punch to the chicken. This roasted chicken will be a great meal for special occasions. Instant pot takes less roasting time for chicken than an oven.

Yield: Makes 6 portions
Cooking Time: 42 minutes

Ingredients

- 1 tablespoon fresh rosemary, minced
- ½ tablespoon ground cumin
- ½ tablespoon cayenne pepper
- ½ tablespoon red pepper flakes, crushed
- Freshly ground black pepper, to taste
- 1 (4-pound) whole chicken, neck and giblets removed
- 2 tablespoons olive oil

Directions

1. In a bowl, mix together rosemary and spices. Generously rub the chicken with the spice mixture.
2. Pour the oil in the Instant Pot and select "Sauté." Add the chicken and cook for about 6-7 minutes or until browned from all sides.
3. Select the "Cancel" button. Next, secure the lid and select "Poultry," using the default time of 20 minutes. Select the "Cancel" button and carefully do a quick release.

4. Remove the lid and flip the side of the chicken. Next, secure the lid and cook under "Manual" and "High Pressure" for about 15 minutes. Select the "Cancel" button and carefully do a quick release.

5. Remove the lid and transfer onto a platter. Keep aside for about 5-10 minutes before slicing.

Braised Turkey Breast

Yield: Makes 8 portions
Cooking Time: 14 minutes

Ingredients

- 1 celery stalk, chopped
- 1 large onion, chopped
- 1 tablespoon fresh thyme, minced
- 1 tablespoon fresh rosemary, minced
- 14-ounce low-sodium chicken broth
- 1 (6½-pound) skin-on, bone-in turkey breast
- Freshly ground black pepper, to taste
- 3 tablespoons cornstarch
- 3 tablespoons water

Directions

1. Arrange a steamer trivet in the Instant Pot. Place the celery, onion, herbs and broth in the Instant Pot. Arrange turkey breast on top and sprinkle with black pepper.
2. Next, secure the lid and cook under "Manual" and "High Pressure" for about 10 minutes. Select the "Cancel" button and carefully do a quick release.
3. Remove the lid and transfer the turkey breast into a bowl. With a slotted spoon, skim off the fat from the surface of the broth and then strain it.
4. In a small bowl, dissolve the cornstarch in water.
5. Return the broth to the Instant Pot and select "Sauté" slowly. Add the cornstarch mixture, stirring

continuously. Cook for about 3-4 minutes. Select the "Cancel" and transfer the gravy into a serving bowl.

6. Cut the turkey breast into desired sized slices and serve alongside the gravy.

Seafood Recipes

Everyone is quite aware of the awe-aspiring health benefits of seafood. The best thing is there is a variety of seafood you can choose from according to your preferences. Along with vegetarian, meats and grain recipes, this book also offers you a variety of healthy and quick seafood recipes to be prepared in Instant Pot.

Citrus Glazed Salmon

This orange juice and wine glazed salmon dish will fill every part of your palate with a depth of flavors. Salmon is known as a nutritionally-dense super food, and it is also an excellent source of high quality minerals, vitamins and protein. Salmon can be prepared in an Instant Pot with little effort.

Yield: Makes 4 plates
Cooking Time: 7 minutes

Ingredients

- 4 (4-ounce) salmon fillets
- 1 teaspoon fresh ginger, minced
- 2 teaspoons fresh orange zest, grated finely
- 1 cup white wine
- 1 tablespoon olive oil
- 3 tablespoons fresh orange juice
- Freshly ground black pepper, to taste

Directions

1. In the Instant Pot, add all ingredients and mix.
2. Next, secure the lid and cook under "Manual" and "High Pressure" for about 7 minutes. Select the "Cancel" button and carefully do a natural release.
3. Remove the lid and serve the salmon fillets topped with the cooking sauce.

Cod & Peas with Wine Sauce

Yield: Makes 4 plates
Cooking Time: 4 minutes

Ingredients

- 4 (4-ounce) cod fillets
- ½ pound frozen peas
- 2 tablespoons fresh parsley
- 2 garlic cloves, chopped
- ½ teaspoon paprika
- 1 cup white wine

Directions

1. Arrange the steamer trivet in the bottom of the Instant Pot. Add 1 cup of the water And arrange the cod fillets in the Instant Pot.

2. Next, secure the lid and cook under "Manual" and "High Pressure" for about 2 minutes. Select the "Cancel" button and carefully do a quick release.

3. Remove the lid and add the peas in the steamer trivet with the cod. Next, secure the lid and cook under "Manual" and "High Pressure" for about 2 minutes. Select the "Cancel" button and carefully do a quick release.

4. Meanwhile in a food processor, add the remaining ingredients and pulse until smooth. Transfer the wine mixture into a bowl. Add cod and peas and stir to combine.

5. Serve immediately.

Cod with Cherry Tomatoes

A cod fish supper with cherry tomatoes that will be great for your dinner table, this meal is packed with delicious flavors. This meal is easy to prepare in an Instant Pot; just place all things in the Instant Pot and wait until the cooking time ends.

Yield: Makes 4 servings
Cooking Time: 5 minutes

Ingredients

- 1 pound cherry tomatoes, halved
- 2 tablespoons fresh rosemary, chopped
- 4 (4-ounce) cod fillets
- 2 garlic cloves, minced
- 1 tablespoon olive oil
- Pinch of salt
- Freshly ground black pepper, to taste

Directions

1. Grease a large heat-proof bowl. Place half of the cherry tomatoes in the bottom of the prepared bowl, followed by the rosemary. Arrange cod fillets on top in a single layer, followed by the remaining tomatoes. Sprinkle with garlic and drizzle with oil. Arrange the bowl into the Instant Pot.

2. Next, secure the lid and cook under "Manual" and "High Pressure" for about 5 minutes. Select the "Cancel" button and carefully do a quick release.

3. Remove the lid and transfer the fish fillets and tomatoes on serving plates. Sprinkle with salt and black pepper, and then serve.

Fish Curry

Yield: Makes 4 servings
Cooking Time: 12 minutes

Ingredients

- 1 tablespoon olive oil
- 2 curry leaves
- 2 medium onions, chopped
- 1 tablespoon fresh ginger, grated finely
- 2 garlic cloves, minced
- 2 tablespoons curry powder
- 2 teaspoons ground cumin
- 2 teaspoons ground coriander
- 1 teaspoon red chili powder
- ½ teaspoon ground turmeric
- 2 cups unsweetened coconut milk
- 1½ pound fish fillets, cut into bite sized pieces
- 1¼ cups tomatoes, chopped
- 1 Serrano pepper, seeded and chopped
- 1 tablespoon fresh lemon juice

Directions

1. Pour the oil in the Instant Pot and select "Sauté." Add the curry leaves and cook for about 30 seconds. Add onion, ginger and garlic, and cook for about 4-5 minutes. Add spices and cook for about 1½ minutes. Stir in the coconut milk. Select "Cancel" and stir in fish, tomatoes and Serrano pepper.

2. Next, secure the lid and cook under "Manual" and "Low Pressure" for about 5 minutes. Select the "Cancel" button and carefully do a natural release.

3. Remove the lid and stir in the lemon juice.

4. Serve hot.

Shrimp with Beans & Veggies

Yield: Makes 8 plates
Cooking Time: 25 minutes

Ingredients

- 3 tablespoons olive oil
- 2 medium onions, chopped
- 1 small green bell pepper, seeded and chopped
- 1 celery stalk, chopped
- 2 garlic cloves, minced
- 2 tablespoons fresh parsley, chopped
- 2 bay leaves
- 1 teaspoon red pepper flakes, crushed
- 1 teaspoon cayenne pepper
- 1 pound great northern beans, rinsed, soaked for overnight and drained
- 2 cups low-sodium chicken broth
- Water, as required
- 1 pound medium shrimp, peeled and deveined

Directions

1. Pour the oil in the Instant Pot and select "Sauté." Add the onion, bell pepper and celery, and cook for about 6 minutes. Add garlic, parsley, bay leaves and spices, and sauté for about 2 minutes. Add beans, broth and the required amount of water to cover the beans.

2. Next, secure the lid and cook under "Manual" and "Medium Pressure" for about 15 minutes. Select the "Cancel" button and carefully do a natural release.

3. Remove and immediately stir in the shrimp. Next, secure the lid and cook under "Manual" and "High Pressure" for about 2 minutes. Select the "Cancel" button and carefully do a quick release. Cover and put aside for at least 10 minutes.

4. Remove the lid and serve hot.

Curried Shrimp

An authentic South Asian-inspired shrimp curry, this subtle dish is richly flavored, as the spices complement the shrimp. Cooking this curry in an Instant Pot is ideal when you are in real hurry. This curry will be great when served with plain rice.

Yield: Makes 6 servings
Cooking Time: 9 minutes

Ingredients

- 1½ tablespoons olive oil
- 1 medium onion, chopped
- 1 teaspoon ground cumin
- 1½ teaspoons red chili powder
- 1 teaspoon ground turmeric
- Pinch of salt
- 2 medium white rose potatoes, cubed
- 4 medium tomatoes, chopped
- ¼ cup water
- 1¾ pound medium shrimp, peeled and deveined
- 1 tablespoon fresh lemon juice
- ¼ cup fresh cilantro, chopped

Directions

1. Pour the oil in the Instant Pot and select "Sauté." Add the onion, bell pepper, carrot, celery and garlic, and cook for about 2-3 minutes. Add spices and cook for about 1 minute. Add potatoes and tomatoes and cook for about 2 minutes. Add water and bring to a gentle simmer. Select "Cancel" and stir in the shrimp.

2. Next, secure the lid and cook under "Manual" and "High Pressure" for about 3 minutes. Select the "Cancel" button and carefully do a natural release.

3. Remove the lid and stir in the lemon juice and cilantro.

4. Serve hot.

Shrimp with Rice

Yield: Makes 4 plates
Cooking Time: 12 minutes

Ingredients

- 1 tablespoon olive oil
- 1½ pounds shrimp, peeled and deveined
- ¼ teaspoon red pepper flakes, crushed and divided
- Pinch of salt
- Freshly ground black pepper, to taste
- 1 small onion, chopped
- 1 large red bell pepper, seeded and
- 2 celery stalks, chopped
- 2 garlic cloves, minced
- 1 jalapeño pepper, seeded and chopped
- 2 cups tomatoes, chopped very finely
- 1 cup long grain white rice
- 1 cup chicken broth
- ¼ cup scallion (green part), chopped

Directions

1. Pour the oil in the Instant Pot and select "Sauté." Then add the shrimp and sprinkle with half the red pepper flakes, a pinch of salt and black pepper. Cook for about 2-3 minutes. Transfer the shrimp into a bowl. Now, add onion, bell pepper and celery, and cook for about 5 minutes. Add garlic, jalapeño, remaining red pepper flakes and black pepper, and sauté for about 1 minute.

Select "Cancel" and stir in the tomatoes, rice and broth, then stir to combine.

2. Next, secure the lid and cook under "Manual" and "High Pressure" for about 8 minutes. Select the "Cancel" button and carefully do a quick release.

3. Remove the lid and immediately stir in the cooked shrimp. Secure the lid right away and keep aside for about 5 minutes before serving.

Buttered Lobster Tails

Yield: Makes 2 plates
Cooking Time: 3 minutes

Ingredients

- 1 cup water
- 2 pound lobster tails, cut in half
- 2 tablespoons unsalted butter, melted
- Pinch of salt

Directions

1. Arrange the steamer trivet in the bottom of the Instant Pot. Add 1 cup of the water in the Instant Pot. Arrange the lobster tails, shell side in the trivet.

2. Next, secure the lid and cook under "Manual" and "Low Pressure" for about 3 minutes. Select the "Cancel" button and carefully do a quick release.

3. Remove the lid and transfer the tails to the serving plate. Drizzle with butter and sprinkle with salt and serve.

Lemony Mussels

Yield: Makes 4 plates
Cooking Time: 6 minutes

Ingredients

- 1 tablespoon olive oil
- 1 medium onion, chopped
- 1 garlic clove, minced
- ½ teaspoon dried rosemary, crushed
- 1 cup low-sodium chicken broth
- 2 tablespoons fresh lemon juice
- Freshly ground black pepper, to taste
- 2 pound mussels, cleaned and de-bearded

Directions

1. Pour the oil in the Instant Pot and select "Sauté." Add the onion and cook for about 5 minutes. Add garlic and rosemary, and sauté for about 1 minute. Select "Cancel" and stir in the broth, lemon juice and black pepper. Place the mussels in steamer trivet and arrange the trivet in the Instant Pot.

2. Next, secure the lid and cook under "Manual" and "Low Pressure" for about 1 minute. Select the "Cancel" button and carefully do a quick release.

3. Remove the lid and transfer the mussels to the serving bowl and top with the cooking liquid from the pot.

4. Serve hot.

Seafood Gumbo

A wonderful dinner recipe of seafood gumbo is considered a classic American meal. Seafood and sausage is cooked in aromatic vegetables, broth and roux. This meal is chock-full of shrimp, crabmeat, scallops and sausages.

Yield: Makes 8 servings
Cooking Time: 22 minutes

Ingredients

- 10 tablespoons olive oil, divided
- 2 red bell peppers, seeded and chopped
- 1 onion, chopped
- 3 celery stalks, chopped
- 4 garlic cloves, minced
- 2 smoked sausages, chopped
- 2 tablespoons dried thyme, crushed
- Freshly ground black pepper, to taste
- 6½ cups low-sodium chicken broth, divided
- ½ cup all-purpose flour
- 1 pound crabmeat
- 1 pound large shrimp, peeled and deveined
- 1 pound scallops

Directions

1. Pour 2 tablespoons of the oil in the Instant Pot and select "Sauté." Add the onion, bell pepper, celery and garlic, and cook for about 5 minutes. Select the

"Cancel" button and stir in the sausage, thyme, black pepper and 6 cups of broth. Stir to combine.

2. Next, secure the lid and cook under "Manual" and "Medium Pressure" for about 10 minutes. Select the "Cancel" button and carefully do a quick release.

3. Meanwhile in a pan, heat the remaining oil on medium-low heat. Add the flour and cook, stirring continuously for about 4-5 minutes. Remove from heat and immediately stir in remaining broth.

4. Remove the lid of the Instant Pot and add the flour mixture and stir till well-combined. Stir in the seafood.

5. Next, secure the lid and cook under "Manual" and "Medium Pressure" for about 2 minutes. Select the "Cancel" button and carefully do a quick release.

6. Remove the lid and serve hot.

Vegetables, Grains & Bean Recipes

Are you vegetarian and looking for meatless recipes? Not a problem. We've got vegetarian recipes here, too. These recipes consist of vegetables, grains and beans, considering your health and taste.

Brussels Sprout Salad

Yield: Makes 4 plates
Cooking Time: 3 minutes

Ingredients

- 1 pound Brussels sprouts, trimmed and halved
- ½ tablespoon unsalted butter, melted
- 1 cup pomegranate seeds
- ¼ cup almonds, chopped

Directions

1. Arrange the steamer trivet in the bottom of the Instant Pot. Add 1 cup of the water. Arrange the Brussels sprouts in the trivet.

2. Next, secure the lid and cook under "Manual" and "High Pressure" for about 3 minutes. Select the "Cancel" button and carefully do a quick release.

3. Remove the lid and transfer the Brussels sprouts to the serving plates. Drizzle with the melted butter. Top with pomegranate seeds and almonds, and then serve.

Lemony Potatoes

A hit recipe for potatoes, these easy to prepare potatoes are phenomenally great. They can be served as a light lunch or as a side dish with any kind of roasted meat alike.

Yield: Makes 4 plates
Cooking Time: 11 minute

Ingredients

- 1 tablespoon olive oil
- 5 medium potatoes, scrubbed and cubed
- 2 tablespoons fresh rosemary, chopped|
- Freshly ground black pepper, to taste
- 1 cup low-sodium vegetable broth
- 2 tablespoons fresh lemon juice

Directions

1. Pour the oil in the Instant Pot and select "Sauté." Add the potatoes, rosemary and black pepper, and cook for about 5 minutes. Select "Cancel" and stir in the broth and lemon juice.
2. Next, secure the lid and cook under "Manual" and "High Pressure" for about 6 minutes. Select the "Cancel" button and carefully do a natural release.
3. Remove the lid and serve warm.

Spinach in Tomato Sauce

Yield: Makes 4 plates
Cooking Time: 11 minute

Ingredients

- 2 tablespoons olive oil
- 1 medium onion, chopped
- 1 tablespoon garlic, minced
- ½ teaspoon red pepper flakes, crushed
- 8 cups fresh spinach, chopped
- 1 cup tomatoes, chopped
- ½ cup homemade tomato puree
- ½ cup white wine
- ¾ cup low-sodium vegetable broth

Directions

1. Pour the oil in the Instant Pot and select "Sauté." Add the onion and cook for about 3 minutes. Add garlic and red pepper flakes and cook for about 1 minute. Add spinach and cook for about 2 minutes. Select "Cancel" and stir in the remaining ingredients.
2. Next, secure the lid and cook under "Manual" and "High Pressure" for about 6 minutes. Select the "Cancel" and carefully do a quick release.
3. Remove the lid and serve warm.

Glazed Carrots

A simple dish of tender carrots with delicious glaze, these carrots have a delish flavoring of mild sweetness and spiciness. Your kids will also enjoy this dish.

Yield: Makes 6 plates
Cooking Time: 5 minute

Ingredients

- 2 pound carrots, peeled and sliced diagonally
- ¼ cup golden raisins
- 1 cup water
- 1 tablespoon unsalted butter, melted
- 1 tablespoon honey
- ¾ teaspoon red pepper flakes, crushed
- Pinch of salt

Directions

1. Place the carrots, raisins and water in the Instant Pot and mix well. Next, secure the lid and cook under "Manual" and "Low Pressure" for about 5 minutes. Select the "Cancel" and carefully do a natural release.
2. Remove the lid and through a strainer, drain the water. Transfer the carrots into a large bowl. Add remaining ingredients and stir to combine well.
3. Serve warm.

Chickpea Curry

Yield: Makes 6 bowls
Cooking Time: 37 minute

Ingredients

- 1 tablespoon olive oil
- 1 onion, chopped
- 1 tablespoon fresh ginger, minced
- 1 tablespoon garlic, minced
- 1 teaspoons curry powder
- 1 teaspoon ground cumin
- ½ teaspoon ground coriander
- 2 medium tomatoes, chopped finely
- 1 cup dried chickpeas, rinsed, soaked for overnight and drained
- 2 cups water
- Pinch of salt
- Freshly ground black pepper, to taste
- ¼ cup fresh parsley, chopped

Directions

1. Pour the oil in the Instant Pot and select "Sauté." Add the onion and cook for about 3 minutes. Add ginger, garlic and spices and cook for about 1 minute. Add tomatoes and cook for about 2 minutes. Select "Cancel" and stir in the chickpeas and water.

2. Next, secure the lid and cook under "Manual" and "High Pressure" for about 20 minutes. Select the "Cancel" button and carefully do a natural release.

3. Remove the lid and stir in salt, black pepper and parsley.
4. Serve hot.

Kidney Beans Curry

When you need a cheap but filling and delicious meal for dinner, this curry will be a great choice for you. It will be a hit for a vegan dinner party because of its deliciousness, but surely this curry would be loved by all.

Yield: Makes 4 bowls
Cooking Time: 37 minute

Ingredients

- 3 cups water
- ¾ cup dried red kidney beans, soaked for overnight and drained
- 2 tablespoons split chickpeas, soaked for overnight and drained
- 2 tablespoons olive oil
- 2 medium onions, chopped
- 2 teaspoons garlic, minced
- 2 teaspoons fresh ginger, minced
- 1 teaspoon ground cumin
- 1 teaspoon ground coriander
- 2 teaspoons red chili powder
- ½ teaspoon ground turmeric
- 1 large tomato, chopped finely
- Pinch of salt
- 3 tablespoons fresh cilantro, chopped

Directions

1. Place the water, beans and split chickpeas in the Instant Pot and mix well. Next, secure the lid and cook under "Manual" and "High Pressure" for about 15 minutes. Select the "Cancel" and carefully do a natural release.

2. Remove the lid and transfer the bean mixture with the cooking liquid into a large bowl. Transfer the ¼ cup of beans and split chickpeas in another bowl and mash them completely.

3. Pour the oil in the Instant Pot and select "Sauté." Add the onion and cook for about 2-3 minutes. Add the garlic, ginger and spices and sauté for about 1 minute. Add tomatoes and cook for about 2 minutes. Select "Cancel" and stir in the mashed and remaining beans mixture.

4. Next, secure the lid and cook under "Manual" and "High Pressure" for about 10-15 minutes. Select the "Cancel" button and carefully do a quick release.

5. Remove the lid and stir in salt and cilantro.

6. Serve hot.

Cheesy & Lemony Rice

Yield: Makes 4 plates
Cooking Time: 3 minute

Ingredients

- 1¼ cups low-sodium vegetable broth
- 1 cup long grain white rice, rinsed
- 1 tablespoon fresh lemon juice
- Freshly ground black pepper, to taste
- 2 tablespoons Parmesan cheese, grated freshly
- 1 teaspoon fresh lemon zest, grated finely
- 2 tablespoons fresh mint leaves, chopped

Directions

1. Place broth, rice, lemon juice and black pepper in the Instant Pot and mix well. Next, secure the lid and cook under "Manual" and "High Pressure" for about 3 minutes. Select the "Cancel" button and carefully do a natural release for about 7 minutes. Then do a quick release.
2. Remove the lid and immediately, stir in the cheese and lemon zest.
3. Serve warm with the garnishing of the mint.

Barley with Mushrooms

Yield: Makes 4 plates
Cooking Time: 30 minute

Ingredients

- 3 tablespoons olive oil, divided
- 1 medium onion, chopped
- 2 garlic cloves, minced
- ½ cup Parmesan cheese, grated and divided
- 1 cup pearl barley
- 2 tablespoons fresh thyme, chopped
- 3 cups low-sodium chicken broth
- 1 pound fresh mushrooms, sliced
- Freshly ground black pepper, to taste
- 2 tablespoons fresh cilantro, chopped

Directions

1. Pour 2 tablespoons of the oil in the Instant Pot and select "Sauté." Then add the onion and cook for about 5 minutes. Add garlic and cook for about 1 minute. Select "Cancel" and stir in the barley, thyme and broth.

2. Next, secure the lid and cook under "Manual" and "High Pressure" for about 25 minutes. Select the "Cancel" button and carefully do a quick release.

3. Meanwhile in a skillet, heat the remaining oil on medium heat. Add mushrooms and sprinkle with black pepper. Cook for about 8-10 minutes.

4. Remove the lid of the Instant Pot and add the cheese and stir until melted completely. Stir in the cooked mushrooms.

5. Serve immediately with the garnishing of cilantro.

Quinoa Pilaf

Yield: Makes 4 plates
Cooking Time: 7 minute

Ingredients

- 1 tablespoon unsalted butter
- 1 celery stalk, chopped finely
- ½ cup onion, chopped
- 14-ounce low-sodium chicken broth
- ¼ cup water
- 1½ cups quinoa, rinsed and drained
- ¼ cup dried cherries
- ½ cup almonds, sliced

Directions

1. Place butter in the Instant Pot and select "Sauté." Add the celery and onion, and cook for about 5 minutes. Add garlic and cook for about 1 minute. Select "Cancel" and stir in the remaining ingredients, except th almonds.
2. Next, secure the lid and cook under "Manual" and "High Pressure" for about 1 minute. Select the "Cancel" button and wait for about 5 minutes. Then, carefully do a quick release.
3. Remove the lid and immediately stir in the almonds.
4. Serve warm.

Creamy Macaroni

An absolutely *amazing supper food for whole family, this simple and delicious Instant Pot recipe is quick to prepare. Prepare this meal for your family and receive plenty of praise. Instant Pot cooking prepares macaroni faster than stovetop cooking.*

Yield: Makes 4 plates
Cooking Time: 8 minute

Ingredients

- 2 cups water
- 1 cup macaroni
- Salt, to taste
- ½ cup milk
- ¼ cup heavy cream
- 2-ounce cream cheese, softened
- 1 tablespoon fresh lemon juice
- 1 tablespoon fresh parsley, chopped finely
- Freshly ground black pepper, to taste

Directions

1. Place water, macaroni and salt in the Instant Pot and mix. Next, secure the lid and cook under "Manual" and "High Pressure" for about 5 minutes. Select the "Cancel" button and wait for about 5 minutes. Then, carefully do a quick release.
2. Remove the lid and select "Sauté" and stir in the milk, heavy cream and cream cheese. Cook for about 2-3 minutes. Select the "Cancel" button and immediately

stir in the lemon juice, parsley and required salt and black pepper.

3. Serve hot.

Dessert Recipes

Talking about deviousness and taste, how one can forget about sweet cravings? No worries, these Instant Pot dessert recipes are healthy and yet wonderfully tasty. Enjoy the purity of natural flavors with heart-warming aroma spreading all over your house.

Glazed Apples

These apples are poached in wine along with demerara sugar and raisins. This yummy and healthy fruit would be a great dessert for barbecue parties.

Yield: Makes 6 portions
Cooking Time: 10 minute

Ingredients

- 6 apples, cored
- 1 cup red wine
- ½ cup demerara sugar
- ¼ cup raisins
- 1 teaspoon ground cinnamon

Directions

1. Place the apples in the Instant Pot. Pour wine on top and sprinkle with sugar, raisins and cinnamon.
2. Next, secure the lid and cook under "Manual" and "High Pressure" for about 10 minutes. Select the "Cancel" and carefully do a quick release.
3. Transfer the apples onto serving plates and top with cooking liquid.

Fudge Cake

Yield: Makes 3 cakes
Cooking Time: 6 minute

Ingredients

- ¼ cup milk
- 2 tablespoons extra-virgin olive oil
- 1 egg
- ¼ cup all-purpose flour
- ¼ cup sugar
- 1 tablespoon cacao powder
- ½ teaspoon baking powder
- 2 teaspoons fresh orange zest, grated finely
- Powdered sugar, as required

Directions

1. Grease 3 ramekins and keep aside.
2. In a bowl, add all ingredients except the powdered sugar and mix until well-combined. Transfer the mixture into the prepared ramekins evenly.
3. Arrange a steamer trivet in the Instant Pot and place 1 cup of the water inside. Arrange the ramekins in the Instant Pot.
4. Next, secure the lid and cook under "Manual" and "High Pressure" for about 6 minutes. Select the "Cancel" button and carefully do a quick release.
5. Remove the lid and transfer the ramekins onto wire racks to cool. Serve with the sprinkling of powdered sugar.

Chocolate Cheesecake

A heavenly cheesecake for dessert lovers, this easy-to-prepare chocolate cheesecake has just the right amount of sweetness. Baking in the Instant Pot takes this cheesecake to a higher level of deliciousness.

Yield: Makes 4 portions
Cooking Time: 18 minute

Ingredients

- 1 egg
- 8-ounce cream cheese, softened
- ¼ cup Swerve (sugar substitute)
- 1 tablespoon powdered peanut butter
- ¾ tablespoon cocoa powder
- ½ teaspoon pure vanilla extract

Directions

1. In a blender, add eggs and cream cheese and pulse until smooth. Add the remaining ingredients and pulse until well-combined. Transfer the mixture into 2 (8-ounce) mason jars evenly.
2. Arrange a steamer trivet in the Instant Pot and place 1 cup of the water inside. Arrange the mason jars in the Instant Pot.
3. Next, secure the lid and cook under "Manual" and "High Pressure" for about 15-18 minutes. Select the "Cancel" button and carefully do a natural release.
4. Remove the lid and transfer the ramekins onto wire racks to cool. Refrigerate to chill for at least 6-8 hours before serving.

Cherry Cheesecake

Yield: Makes 6 portions
Cooking Time: 40 minute

Ingredients

For Filling

- 8-ounce cream cheese, softened
- 8-ounce ricotta cheese
- ¼ cup powdered sugar
- 2 eggs
- ¼ cup sour cream
- 1 tablespoon vanilla extract

For Crust

- 10 Oreo cookies, crushed
- 2 tablespoons unsalted butter, melted

For Topping

- 2 tablespoons powdered sugar
- ¼ cup fresh cherries, pitted

Directions

1. In a bowl, add cream cheese, ricotta, sugar and eggs and beat until smooth. Fold in sour cream and vanilla extract. In another bowl, mix together crushed Oreo cookies and butter. Place the cookie mixture evenly in the bottom of a 7-inch springform pan and gently press

down to smooth the surface. Evenly top with the cheese mixture.

2. Arrange a steamer trivet in the Instant Pot and place 1 cup of the water inside. Arrange the pan in the Instant Pot.

3. Next, secure the lid and cook under "Manual" and "High Pressure" for about 40 minutes. Select the "Cancel" button and carefully do a quick release.

4. Remove the lid and transfer the ramekins onto wire racks to cool. Refrigerate to chill for at least 12 hours before serving.

5. Sprinkle with cherries and top with cherries before serving.

Tapioca Pudding

Yield: Makes 4 bowls
Cooking Time: 9 minute

Ingredients

- 1½ cups water
- ½ cup small pearl tapioca
- ½ cup sugar
- Pinch of salt
- ½ cup milk
- 2 egg yolks
- ½ teaspoon vanilla extract
- ¼ cup fresh raspberries

Directions

1. Place water and tapioca in the Instant Pot and mix. Next, secure the lid and cook under "Manual" and "High Pressure" for about 6 minutes. Select the "Cancel" button and carefully do a natural release for about 10 minutes. Then do a quick release.

2. Remove the lid and stir in the sugar and salt.

3. In a bowl, add the milk and egg yolks and beat well. Through a fine mesh strainer, pour the milk mixture into the Instant Pot.

4. Now, select "Sauté" and cook for about 2-3 minutes, stirring continuously. Stir in vanilla extract and select the "Cancel" button.

5. Transfer the pudding into serving bowls and refrigerate to chill completely. Serve with the garnishing of raspberries.

Rice Pudding

Yield: Makes 4 bowls
Cooking Time: 10 minute

Ingredients

- 1½ cups unsweetened vanilla almond milk
- 1½ cups water
- 1 cup jasmine rice
- ¼ cup raw sugar
- ¼ raisins
- 1 teaspoon vanilla extract
- 1 teaspoon ground cinnamon
- Pinch of salt
- ¼ cup walnuts, chopped

Directions

1. Place all ingredients except walnuts in the Instant Pot and mix.

2. Next, secure the lid and select "Rice" and just use the default time of 10 minutes. Select the "Cancel" button and carefully do a quick release.

3. Remove the lid and transfer into serving bowls. Top with walnuts and serve warm.

Bread Pudding

If you are looking for a classic dessert for your family, then prepare this delicious bread pudding. This delicious bread pudding is prepared in the Instant Pot in just 20 minutes. Surely your family would like this dessert.

Yield: Makes 8 portions
Cooking Time: 20 minutes

Ingredients

- 3 cups milk
- 4 tablespoons unsalted butter, melted
- ½ cup packed brown sugar
- 3 eggs
- ½ teaspoon ground cinnamon
- 1 teaspoon vanilla extract
- Pinch of salt
- 7 (¾-inch thick) bread slices, cubed and toasted
- ½ cup raisins
- ¼ cup pecans, chopped

Directions

1. In a large bowl, add the milk, butter, brown sugar, eggs, cinnamon, vanilla extract and salt, and beat until well-combined. Add the bread cubes and raisins, and gently stir to combine. Keep aside for about 20 minutes, stirring occasionally. Transfer the mixture into a glass baking dish that fits in the Instant Pot. With a large piece of foil, cover the baking dish.

2. Arrange a steamer trivet in the Instant Pot and place 1½ cups of the water. Arrange the baking dish in the Instant Pot.

3. Next, secure the lid and cook under "Manual" and "High Pressure" for about 20 minutes. Select the "Cancel" button and carefully do a quick release.

4. Remove the lid and transfer the baking dish onto a wire rack to cool slightly.

5. Serve warm with the topping of pecans.

Vanilla Flan

Yield: Makes 8 portions
Cooking Time: 9 minutes

Ingredients

- 4 large eggs
- 1 cup milk
- 1 can sweetened condensed milk
- ¾ cup water
- 1 teaspoon vanilla extract
- Pinch of salt
- ½ cup maple syrup

Directions

1. In a large bowl, add the eggs and beat well. Add the remaining ingredients except maple syrup and mix until well-combined. Spread a thin layer of maple syrup in a glass baking dish that fits in the Instant Pot. Place the egg mixture over the maple syrup layer evenly.

2. Arrange a steamer trivet in the Instant Pot and place 1 cup of the water inside. Arrange the baking dish in the Instant Pot.

3. Next, secure the lid and cook under "Manual" and "High Pressure" for about 9 minutes. Select the "Cancel" button and carefully do a natural release for about 10 minutes. Then carefully do a quick release.

4. Remove the lid and transfer the baking dish onto a wire rack to cool slightly. With plastic wrap, cover the baking dish and refrigerate to chill for about 3 hours.

Crème Brûlée

This super easy recipe of a delicious crème Brûlée is a dessert with excellent texture and flavor. This wonderfully delicious dessert is great to serve at dinner parties.

Yield: Makes 4 portions
Cooking Time: 13 minutes

Ingredients

- 2 cups heavy cream
- 5 egg yolks
- ½ cup sugar
- 1 tablespoon vanilla extract
- ¼ cup superfine sugar

Directions

1. In a bowl, add all ingredients except superfine sugar and beat till well-combined. Divide the mixture in 4 (6-ounce) ramekins evenly.

2. Arrange a steamer trivet in the Instant Pot and place 2 cups of the water inside. Arrange the ramekins on a trivet.

3. Next, secure the lid and cook under "Manual" and "High Pressure" for about 13 minutes. Select the "Cancel" and carefully do a natural release.

4. Remove the lid and transfer the baking dish onto a wire rack to cool for about 30 minutes. With a plastic wrap, cover the ramekins and refrigerate to chill for about 4 hours.

5. Just before serving, sprinkle superfine sugar over each ramekin evenly.

6. Holding th kitchen torch about 2-inches above the surface of the custard, caramelize the sugar.

7. Serve immediately.

Apple Crisp

A perfect dessert recipe when apples are abundant in season, this dessert would be great for special occasions and parties. Surely you will make this recipe again and again.

Yield: Makes 8 portions
Cooking Time: 9 minutes

Ingredients

- 5 medium apples, peeled, cored and chopped
- 2 teaspoons ground cinnamon
- ¼ teaspoon ground ginger
- ¼ teaspoon ground nutmeg
- 1 tablespoon pure maple syrup
- ½ cup water
- ¾ cup old-fashioned rolled oats
- ¼ cup flour
- ¼ cup brown sugar
- ¼ cup unsalted butter, melted
- Pinch of salt

Directions

1. In a bowl, mix together the oats, flour, brown sugar, butter and salt. Place the chopped apples in the Instant Pot and sprinkle with the spices. Place the maple syrup and water over the apples evenly. Evenly top with the oats mixture.

2. Next, secure the lid and cook under "Manual" and "High Pressure" for about 8 minutes. Select the "Cancel" button and carefully do a natural release.

3. Remove the lid and transfer the baking dish onto a wire rack to cool slightly. Serve warm.

Conclusion

Remember, this is your first step to a healthier and more energetic life. Once you get full command over using your Instant Pot, you can prepare any food of your choice, and you can customize the recipes according to your taste. Eat healthy and stay healthy!

I wanted to show my appreciation that you support my work so I've put together a free gift for you.

LINK TO YOUR FREE GIFT

Just visit the link above to download it now.

I know you will love this gift.

Thanks!

Julia Nelson

Made in the USA
Middletown, DE
24 September 2018